dabblelab

10-MINUTE
UPCYCLED
PROJECTS

BY TAMMY ENZ

CAPSTONE PRESS
a capstone imprint

Dabble Lab is published by Capstone Press, an imprint of Capstone.
1710 Roe Crest Drive, North Mankato, Minnesota 56003
www.capstonepub.com

Library of Congress Cataloging-in-Publication Data
Names: Enz, Tammy, author.
Title: 10-minute upcycled projects / Tammy Enz.
Other titles: Ten-minute upcycled projects
Description: North Mankato, Minnesota : Capstone Press, 2021. | Series: 10-minute makers | Includes bibliographical references. | Audience: Ages 8–9 | Audience: Grades 2–3 | Summary: "Looking for clever ideas to reuse and recycle the materials in your makerspace? You're in luck! From earbud bracelets and bottle cap fireflies to tin man wind chimes and cell phone sleeves, these amazing 10-minute upcycled projects will have kids making in no time!"—Provided by publisher.
Identifiers: LCCN 2020003364 (print) | LCCN 2020003365 (ebook) | ISBN 9781496680914 (library binding) | ISBN 9781496680969 (ebook pdf)
Subjects: LCSH: Handicraft—Juvenile literature. | Recycled products—Juvenile literature. | Resourcefulness—Juvenile literature.
Classification: LCC TT160 .E5844 2021 (print) | LCC TT160 (ebook) | DDC 745.5—dc23
LC record available at https://lccn.loc.gov/2020003364
LC ebook record available at https://lccn.loc.gov/2020003365

Photo Credits
All photographs by Capstone: Karon Dubke; Marcy Morin and Sarah Schuette, Project Production; Heidi Thompson, Art Director

Design Elements
Shutterstock: balabolka, casejustin, H Art, Jenov Jenovallen, KannaA, nichy, sergio34, Tanya Sun, Vikoshkina, Vintage Love Story, Yes - Royalty Free, Zebra Finch

Editorial Credits
Editor: Christopher Harbo; Designer: Tracy McCabe; Media Researcher: Tracy Cummins; Production Specialist: Katy LaVigne

All internet sites appearing in back matter were available and accurate when this book was sent to press.

TABLE OF CONTENTS

GOT 10 MINUTES?

Raid your closet. Dig through your recycling bin. Empty your drawers. In no time, you'll have everything you need to make more than a dozen fun upcycled projects. Even better, with just a few simple steps, these cool projects will come together super-fast. You'll even have time for cleaning up!

General Supplies and Tools

acrylic paint

cardboard

cord

craft sticks

decoupage glue

disposable cup

electrical tape

glitter

glue stick

googly eyes

hammer and nail

hole punch

hot glue gun

magazines

markers

metal washers

pipe cleaners

ruler

scissors

string

tin cans

toothpicks

utility knife

yarn

Tips

- Gather all of your supplies before starting a project.

- There's no right or wrong way to make these projects! Experiment and use your imagination.

- Ask an adult to help you with sharp or hot tools.

- Add your own flair! Make each creation unique by adding your own ideas.

EARBUD BRACELET

Don't toss broken earbud cords. Use them to whip up this cool and colorful bracelet.

What You Need:

2 broken earbud cords
scissors
ruler
tape
small beads

What You Do:

1 Peel apart and cut the cords into three pieces, each 30 inches (76 centimeters) long.

2 Line up the cords and fold them in half.

3 Pull out the folded end of one cord to make a small loop. Tie the other cords around the loop.

4 Tape the loop to a table. Then braid the cords by overlapping them one after another. Every four to six braids, thread small beads onto one of the cords.

5 Keep braiding until the bracelet fits around your wrist. Tie the end of the cords into a knot. Trim down the loose ends.

6 Remove the tape. Thread the knot through the loop to finish the bracelet.

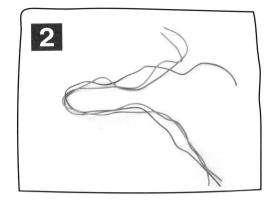

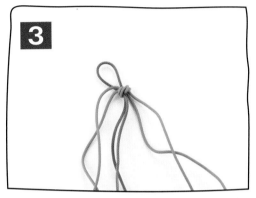

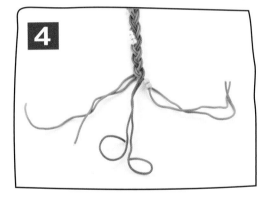

TIP Braid colorful string or yarn into your bracelet to add extra pops of color.

WEARABLE WASHERS

Metal washers are not just for the workshop.
Glam them up with permanent markers to
make this nifty necklace.

What You Need:

4–8 metal washers, different sizes
permanent markers
3–7 small paper clips
24-inch- (61-cm-) long cord
scissors

What You Do:

1. Decorate one side of each washer with permanent markers. Blow on them to dry.

2. Arrange the washers in a fun pattern.

3. Connect the washers with small paper clips.

4. Tie one end of the cord to one side of your washer arrangement.

5. Thread the loose end of the cord through a washer on the other side of the washer arrangement. Pinch the cord tight and put the necklace on.

6. Adjust the loose cord until you like the length of the necklace. Then tie it in place and cut off any extra cord.

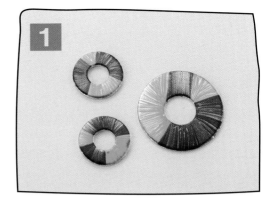

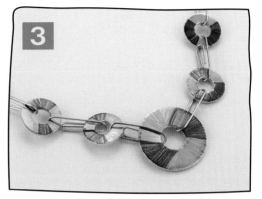

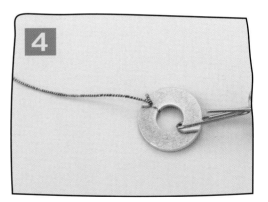

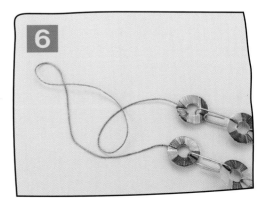

KITTY LANTERN

Rescue a milk jug from your recycling bin.
Then upcycle it into this cute kitty to light
up your yard or room.

What You Need:

large milk jug
utility knife
markers
felt
scissors
hot glue gun
2 pipe cleaners
colored tissue paper
battery-powered tea light

What You Do:

1 Ask an adult to cut off the milk jug's spout and handle with the utility knife.

2 Draw a kitty nose, eyes, and mouth on one side of the jug.

3 Cut the felt into shapes that look like cat ears. Glue them above the kitty's face.

4 Fold each pipe cleaner in half. Then glue them on either side of the nose to make whiskers.

5 Fill the inside of the jug with tissue paper.

6 Turn on the tea light and nest it inside the tissue paper.

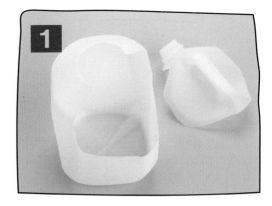

TIP What other kinds of animals can you make? Try making a puppy, turkey, or bear.

FIREFLY FRIEND

Brighten your day every time you
open your locker with a firefly friend.
It's charming and easy to make.

What You Need:

plastic water bottle
scissors
hot glue gun
metal bottle cap
2 googly eyes
LED bulb
CR2032 button battery
electrical tape
button magnet

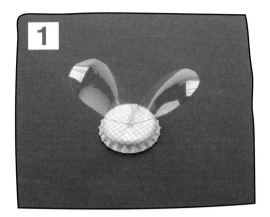

What You Do:

1. Cut a small pair of wings out of the water bottle. Hot glue them to the top of the bottle cap.

2. Glue the googly eyes to the bottle cap right below the wings.

3. Slide the LED onto the button battery. The short wire should touch the negative (-) side. The long wire should touch the positive (+) side. Wrap a short piece of electrical tape around the battery to keep the LED in place.

4. Glue the battery inside the bottle cap so the LED stands up behind the wings.

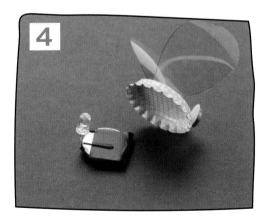

5. Place the bottle cap on the magnet.

6. Stick the firefly on your locker for a fun glowing friend.

TIP To turn off the firefly, remove the magnet and slide one of the LED leads out from under the tape.

13

CRAYON CREATION

What can you do with short and broken crayons? Break them up even more to make a colorful design of the first letter in your name!

What You Need:

cardboard (any size)
pencil
old crayons
scissors
hot glue gun

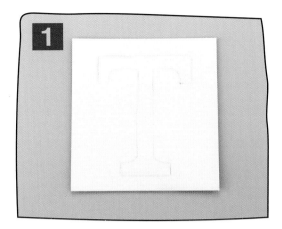

What You Do:

1. Lightly sketch a large letter on the cardboard.

2. Pick out a variety of crayons and peel off their paper wrappers.

3. Break the crayons into pieces that will cover the letter's shape. To make small pieces, cut through the crayons with scissors.

4. Lay out the crayons on top of the letter.

5. Once arranged, remove the crayon pieces one at a time. Carefully hot glue each piece in place.

TIP Try making other colorful designs with crayons, such as flowers or hearts.

BFF PUZZLE
NECKLACES

A puzzle isn't much fun when a piece goes missing. But don't despair. Just turn the remaining pieces into one-of-a-kind friendship necklaces!

What You Need:

3 connecting puzzle pieces
markers
hole punch
3 24-inch- (61-cm-) long cords

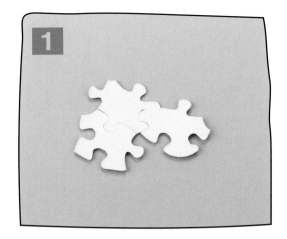

What You Do:

1 Connect the puzzle pieces and flip them over.

2 Use the markers to create a design or message across the back of all the pieces.

3 Punch a hole in the top of each puzzle piece.

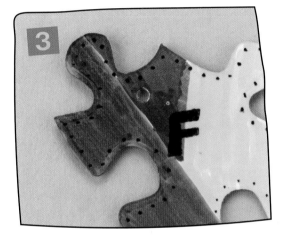

4 Separate the puzzle pieces and thread a cord onto each one. Tie the ends of each cord to make necklaces.

5 Give the necklaces to your best friends!

TIP Boost team spirit! Make enough connecting necklaces for the teammates of a sport you play.

TIN MAN
WIND CHIME

Don't leave tin cans clanging around in your
recycling bin. Use a couple to whip up this little
tin man wind chime.

What You Need:

tall tin can
short tin can
hammer
nail
24-inch (61-cm)
   piece of yarn
4 5-inch (13-cm)
   pieces of yarn
9 metal washers
ruler
toothpick
hot glue gun
2 googly eyes
marker

What You Do:

1. Ask an adult to punch a hole in the top of each can with the hammer and nail.

2. Fold the 24-inch (61-cm) piece of yarn in half and tie its loose ends to a washer. About 2 inches (5 cm) up from the washer, tie a triple knot in the long loop of yarn.

3. Thread the yarn above the knot through the tall can, and then up through the short can. Use a toothpick to help push the yarn through the holes.

4. Tie washers onto the ends of the remaining pieces of yarn.

5. Hot glue one washer from each piece of yarn to the bottom can to make arms and legs.

6. Hot glue the googly eyes and draw a mouth on the top can to complete your tin man wind chime.

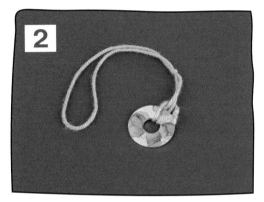

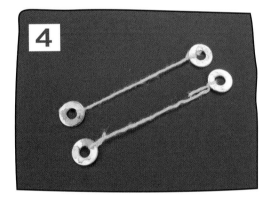

T-SHIRT PILLOW

Do you have a favorite T-shirt that doesn't fit anymore? Don't toss it! Turn it into a no-sew pillow to jazz up your room.

What You Need:

T-shirt
scissors
ruler
fiberfill stuffing

What You Do:

1 Lay the T-shirt on a flat surface. Cut off the arms, bottom hem, and neck of the shirt to create two identical rectangles.

2 Keeping the rectangles stacked flat, cut 3-inch (8-cm) squares out of each corner.

3 Beginning near one corner, cut 3-inch- (8-cm-) deep slits evenly on all four edges of both layers. Space each slit about 1 inch (2.5 cm) apart.

4 Keeping the fabric stacked, tie each tab, one after another, into a double knot.

5 When only six tabs remain, stuff fiberfill though the opening to fill the pillow.

6 Once stuffed, finish tying the remaining tabs.

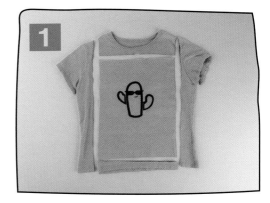

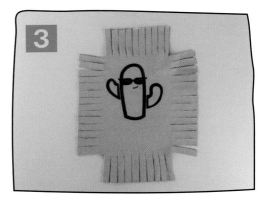

TIP Sweatshirt fabric or old fleece blankets work well for this project too!

POURED PAINT LUMINARY

It's easy to add a splash of color to an old jar.
With some glitter and lights, this luminary will
really make your room glow.

What You Need:

craft stick
1 tablespoon (15 mL) decoupage
   glue
1 teaspoon (5 mL) water
food coloring
disposable cup
glass jar
glitter
battery-powered fairy lights

What You Do:

1 Use a craft stick to mix together the decoupage glue, water, and 15 drops of food coloring in a disposable cup.

2 Pour the mixture into the glass jar. Add a few sprinkles of glitter.

3 Swirl the mixture around in the jar to coat the inside.

4 Pour any excess mixture back into the disposable cup and throw away.

5 Wait a couple minutes as the decoupage glue dries very quickly. Once dry, add the fairy lights to the jar.

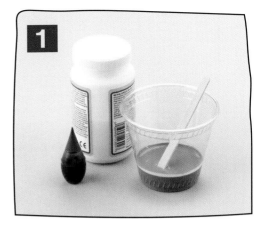

PINWHEEL COLLAGE

Don't throw out your old magazines.
Turn their glossy pages into colorful art!

What You Need:

magazine
scissors
ruler
hot glue gun
6-inch- (15-cm-) long string

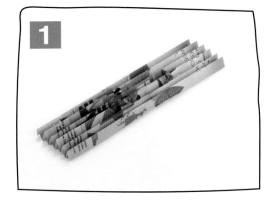

What You Do:

1 Cut a page from the magazine. Accordion fold it along one of its long edges by making creases every 0.5 inch (1 cm).

2 Fold the creased page in half. Glue the edges that meet together to make a fan.

3 Repeat steps 1 and 2 to make two more fans.

4 Glue the edges of the three fans together to make a pinwheel.

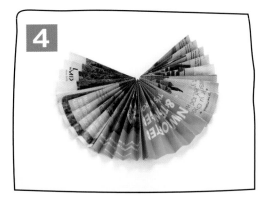

5 Repeat steps 1 through 4 to make several more pinwheels. Make smaller pinwheels by accordion folding the short edges of the magazine pages.

6 Glue the pinwheels together to make a colorful collage. Then loop a string and glue it to the top of the collage so it can hang.

TIP Try different types of paper for this project. Book pages and wrapping paper work well too.

CELL PHONE SLEEVE

Check your closets for a long—forgotten necktie. Then upcycle the colorful castoff into a stylish cell phone case.

What You Need:

old necktie
ruler
scissors
hot glue gun
self-adhesive hook and loop
  fasteners

What You Do:

1 Cut off the wide end of the necktie 14 inches (36 cm) from its tip. Set the rest of the tie aside.

2 Open the flaps on the back of the tie. Fold the top edge down 0.5 inch (1 cm) and glue in place.

3 Place your phone in the center of the tie. Fold the bottom edge up and top edge down to create a pocket. Remove the phone and glue the center seam in place.

4 Tuck the cut edge of the tie inside the pocket and glue the opening closed.

5 Stick the fasteners to the inside of the tip and the face of the case to make a closable flap.

6 Cut the narrow end of the tie 9 inches (23 cm) from its tip. Glue the ends together to make a loop.

7 Glue the end of the loop about 1 inch (2.5 cm) below the back of the case's top edge.

TIP Slide your cell phone into the case and hang it in your locker.

27

SNOWFLAKE ORNAMENT

Raid the recycling bin for cardboard tubes. Then make them into a bunch of beautiful snowflakes.

What You Need:

cardboard tube
ruler
pencil
scissors
hot glue gun
glue stick
glitter
6-inch- (15-cm-) long string

What You Do:

1. Flatten the cardboard tube. Mark lines every 0.25 inch (0.6 cm) along the flattened edge with a pencil.

2. Cut along the lines from step 1 to make oval slices.

3. Arrange four slices in a star pattern. Hot glue the points at the center to form a basic snowflake shape.

4. Fold four more slices in half. Fit each folded slice between a main section of the snowflake shape. Hot glue them at the center.

5. Rub glue stick onto the face of the snowflake. Dip the face of the snowflake into a pile of glitter.

6. Tie a string in a loop around one point of the snowflake to hang.

TIP Just like real snowflakes, the designs you can create are unlimited. Layer the ovals or slice them in half to make different designs.

PERFECT PAINTED PLANTER

What can you do with a used water bottle? Pamper your plants with the perfect painted planter!

What You Need:

plastic bottle
utility knife
acrylic paint
paintbrush
hole punch
12-inch- (30-cm-) long string
soil and plant

What You Do:

1 Ask an adult to cut off the bottom third of the plastic bottle with a utility knife. Recycle the top of the bottle.

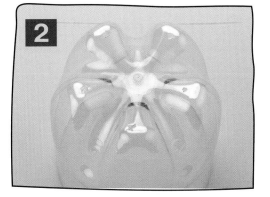

2 Ask an adult to poke several holes in the bottom of the bottle with the utility knife for drainage.

3 Decorate the bottom of the bottle with fun designs using acrylic paint. Blow on the paint to help it dry quickly.

4 Punch holes on opposite sides of the planter. Tie the string to the holes so the planter can hang.

5 Fill the bottom of the bottle with soil and plant your favorite plant in it.

TIP Hang this planter outdoors so water can freely drain from the holes in the bottom.

Read More

Harbo, Christopher L., and Sarah L. Schuette. *Make Art with Circuits.* North Mankato, MN: Capstone Press, 2020.

Kington, Emily. *I Am Not a Paper Roll!* Minneapolis: Hungry Tomato, 2018.

Thompson, Veronica. *Earth-Friendly Earth Day Crafts*. Minneapolis: Lerner Publications, 2019.

Internet Sites

Recycling Crafts for Kids
www.glad.com/teachable-trash/recycling-crafts-for-kids

Totally Awesome Upcycle Crafts for Kids
www.paper-and-glue.com/2015/04/totally-awesome-upcycle-crafts-for-kids.html

Upcycled Crafts for Kids
www.parentmap.com/article/upcycled-crafts-for-kids-and-families